OTHER BOOKS BY ALEX MITCHELL

Quizzin' Nine-Nine: A *Brooklyn Nine-Nine* Quiz Book

Parks & Interrogation: A *Parks & Recreation* Quiz Book

Q & AC-12: A *Line of Duty* Quiz Book

Know Your Schitt: A *Schitt's Creek* Quiz Book

Examilton: A *Hamilton* Quiz Book

Stranger Thinks: A *Stranger Things* Quiz Book

The El Clued Brothers: A *Peep Show* Quiz Book

Dunder Quizlin: An *Office US* Quiz Book

A Question of Succession: A *Succession* Quiz Book

The Big Bang Queries: A *Big Bang Theory* Quiz Book

The Greendale Study Guide: A *Community* Quiz Book

Know Your Schmidt: A *New Girl* Quiz Book

Les Quizérables: *A Les Misérables* Quiz Book

Dunce or Dunphy? A *Modern Family* Quiz Book

Top of the Classo

A *Ted Lasso* Quiz Book

Published by Beartown Press

ISBN: 9798491947300

"Guys underestimated me my entire life. And for years, I never understood why. It used to really bother me. But then one day I was driving my little boy to school and I saw this quote by Walt Whitman and it was painted on the wall there. It said: 'Be curious, not judgmental.' And I liked that. So I get back in my car and I'm driving to work, and all of a sudden it hits me. All them fellas that used to be belittle me; not a single one of them were curious. They thought they had everything all figured out. So they judged everything, and everyone. And I realized that their underestimating me...who I was had nothing to do with it. Cause if they were curious, they could've asked questions. You know? Questions like: 'Have you played a lot of darts, Ted' To which I would've answered: 'Yes, sir. Every Sunday afternoon at a sports bar with my father, from age ten 'til I was 16, when he passed away.' Barbecue sauce."

--Ted Lasso

Contents

Introduction

What a delight *Ted Lasso* is. For a fish-out-of-water comedy about an American football coach who moves to England to manage an underperforming "soccer" team, the show delivers a crazy amount of heart and truth bombs within its runtime.

I read an interview with co-creator Bill Lawrence in which he discussed the idea of mentors being the core of the show. Frequently individual characters like Roy find themselves cast as both the mentor and the mentored as they go on their own personal journey to evolve.

But beyond all of that *Ted Lasso* is simply a fantastic show, and so it felt only right to create a quiz book in its honour. Here's what you'll be lining up against inside these pages:

- More than 250 questions (and, crucially, answers) about *Ted Lasso*.

- Those questions are split into 25 themed rounds, including a final set of tiebreakers to separate the Diamond Dogs from the rest of the pack.

- If you've not seen all of the *Ted Lasso* yet, you will likely come across the odd spoiler.

So, ready to kick off a game of *Top of the Classo*? Let's get started.

Ted

1. By the end of the opening credits, in which letter of his own name is Ted seen to be sitting in the stand?

2. Ted's first match as Richmond coach takes place against which team?

3. Which US state is Ted from?

4. What is Ted's son's name?

5. What did Ted give his son for Christmas in season two?

6. What is the name of his ex-wife, from whom he divorced during season two?

7. Which team are Richmond playing against in the FA Cup when Ted suffers a panic attack?

8. Which popular British sport did Ted claim sounded like a brand of cookies?

9. Which university football team was Ted coaching before he joined Richmond?

10. Which condiment did Ted reference, right before throwing his final dart to beat Rupert in their pub match?

Answers on page 63

Roy

1. What part of Roy's features did a photographer describe as "crazy"?

2. What is Roy's niece's name?

3. What was the first professional club Roy played for after graduating from their youth team?

4. Which club was Roy playing for when he won the Champions League?

5. What was the name of the book Ted gave to Roy in order to coax out his leadership skills?

6. Which book did he later become obsessed with due to its very short chapters?

7. Roy spends an afternoon with his niece's teacher in the penultimate episode of season two. What is her name?

8. Who does Roy select to replace him as the team's captain?

9. What are Roy's favourite flowers, once sent to him by Jamie Carragher?

10. Ted left tickets for Roy each game under an alias of famous country and rock singers. When Roy finally turned up to take his role as coach, what name were the tickets held under?

Answers on page 64

Nate

1. What is Nate's job at the start of season one?

2. What is the name of the restaurant at which Nate wishes to get his parents the window table for their anniversary?

3. What type of car does Nate drive in season one?

4. Nate says that his dad used to be a cartographer. How tall did he used to say Nate was?

5. After Ted suffers a panic attack in the FA Cup match, Nate makes a triple substitution and instructs the team to do what?

6. What becomes Nate's nickname after a misspeak in the post-match interview following that game?

7. What item does Ted gift to Nate in recognition of his promotion to coach?

8. Nate books a restaurant table for his parents' wedding anniversary. Which anniversary was it?

9. What animal did Nate say he would like to be reincarnated as?

10. Who does Nate invite to help him shop for a new suit during season two?

Answers on page 65

Beard

1. What song does Beard sing when the squad performs karaoke after the Everton match?

2. While blending in at the member's club, Beard pretends to be an Irish professor from which university?

3. Which two football pundits does Beard hallucinate to be commenting on his mental health during their post-match analysis?

4. What is the name of Beard's main love interest in the first two seasons?

5. What game is Beard able to play against her without the aid of any of the typical equipment?

6. What is Beard's mother's first name?

7. What does Beard say is the "perfect" amount of nights to spend in Vegas?

8. What act does Beard describe as being like "reading an instruction manual as to why [a person] is nuts"?

9. Which two things is Beard allergic to?

10. Where did Beard spend Christmas in season two?

Answers on page 66

Keeley

1. What type of animal did Keeley dress as in a photoshoot to promote a brand of coffee-flavoured vodka in season one?

2. What was the other option?

3. Which city did Keeley take part in an infomercial for, which unfortunately was shown on all TVs in the team hotel for an away game?

4. What TV show was Keeley watching when she snapped at Roy to give her more space?

5. What footage of Roy does Keeley find extremely attractive?

6. Which magazine ran a business issue profile that declared Keeley "a powerful woman on the rise"?

7. Which is the only room in the stadium where Keeley and Rebecca decide that smoking "doesn't count"?

8. What name does Keeley give to her and Roy's "adult" plan for the festive season, in which they'll get dressed up, sip martinis and sit by the fire?

9. When consoling Roy's niece, Keeley tells her that problems are like which vegetable?

10. What type of business was Keeley advertising when she jumped out of a plane topless while eating a hamburger, as recounted by Roy?

Answers on page 67

Sam

1. Which country is Sam from?

2. What song did Sam perform when the squad did karaoke after the Everton game?

3. Which actress does Sam admire for her pitch-perfect accent and her "grossly underrated" gift for physical comedy?

4. What is Sam's username on the dating app on which he connects with Rebecca?

5. Which part of London does Sam live in, as seen when he texts Rebecca his address?

6. What is his favourite food?

7. Which book series is Sam a fan of?

8. And what is his favourite film?

9. Ted shifts Sam into a midfield position soon after he takes over the team, allowing Sam to contribute more in attack, but what position is Sam playing when Ted first arrives?

10. What does Sam do with the green army man given to him by Ted?

Answers on page 68

Rebecca

1, What is Rebecca's username on the dating app on which she connects with Sam?

2. What was the name of the restaurant Rebecca went to with Sam on their first date?

3. What song does Rebecca perform when the squad go to sing karaoke after the Everton match?

4. And what song does she sing in the eulogy at her father's funeral?

5. What is Flo's nickname for Rebecca?

6. What fundraising event did Rebecca host in season one?

7. Which singer was originally planned to sing at the fundraiser, before Rupert apparently encouraged them to cancel?

8. What do the press begin to refer to Rebecca as, once Rupert's new girlfriend Bex emerges on the scene?

9. What mode of transport do Rebecca and Keeley take after the fundraiser in series one?

10. What is Rebecca's mother's name?

Answers on page 69

Jamie

1. Which club loaned Jamie to Richmond during season one?

2. What shirt number did Jamie wear when playing against Richmond for his parent club?

3. What is Jamie's dad's name?

4. Jamie claims that he realised he had to stop waiting for life to begin and living life to the fullest after the death of whom?

5. What is the signal given to Jamie by the Richmond coaching staff when they want him to play more selfishly?

6. What was the name of the island-based reality dating show on which Jamie appeared after his initial loan spell at Richmond?

7. What did Jamie put in the box intended for donations to buy a gift for Sam to boost his confidence?

8. What is Jamie drinking in the nightclub when Roy confronts him and the rest of the group about bullying Nate?

9. What is the name of the beer for which Jamie is an ambassador?

10. Jamie has a Chinese tattoo on his arm. What does it translate to?

Answers on page 70

Higgins

1. What was Higgins' job at AFC Richmond at the start of *Ted Lasso*?

2. What is Higgins' first name?

3. What musical instrument does Higgins play?

4. How many children does Higgins have?

5.. What is the occupation of Higgins' eldest son?

6. Higgins once wrote a play about a billionaire who took a footballer to a museum and then dinner. Why did the characters get their meal for free?

7. Higgins was the only child in his primary school to suffer from which condition?

8. What does Higgins say is the technical name for the beard he sports towards the end of season one, which his wife hates with a "white-hot intensity"?

9. What is the name of Higgins' wife?

10. What is Higgins' ringtone for his wife?

Answers on page 71

General Knowledge

1. Which country is star striker Dani Rojas from?

2. Which newspaper does reporter Trent Crimm work for?

3. What is the name of the Ghanaian billionaire who attempts to sign Sam?

4. And which African team is that billionaire intending to buy?

5. What song does Ted have the team practicing a dance to for Sharon's leaving party?

6. What is the name of the pub frequented by Ted, Beard and a number of Richmond fans?

7. And what is the name of the pub's landlady?

8. Whose birthday is celebrated after a defeat in season one?

9. What is Rebecca's nickname for her friend Flo?

10. What is the name of the problem-solving task force established by Ted, consisting of himself, Beard, Nate and Higgins?

Answers on page 72

Anagrams

1. A Noisy Samba?

2. Tory Ken?

3. A Jam Titter?.

4. Charade Cob?

5. So Salted?

6. A Concrete Blew?

7. Eek Enjoys El?

8. A Prominent Urn?

9. Siege Shilling?

10. Heal Tensely?

11. Mr Cent Trim?

12. Net Foolhardiness?

13. Fills Colon?

14. Aide Wok Fun?

15. Hyena Ruler Dog?

Answers on page 73

Trick Plays

Can you pick the real trick plays considered by Richmond in series one, and identify the ones we've made up?

1. The Belgian Deadline?

2. Beckham's Todger?

3. Code Beaujolais?

4. Frightshaft?

5. Lasso Special?

6. Loki's Toboggan?

7. Hadrian's Wall?

8. The Broken Tap?

9. The Upside Down Taxi?

10. Nakatomi Plaza?

11. The Satin Chokey?

12. Chitty Chitty Bang Bang?

13. The Jealous Heron?

14. Land of Hope and Glory?

15. Midnight Poutine?

16. The Baffler?

17. Rupert's Lament?

18. Dirty Martini?

19. Gentle Bailiff?

20. The Queen's Gambit?

Answers on page 75

General Knowledge

1. What is the name of Rupert and Bex's baby?

2. Why is Bex able to calm the baby so easily?

3. What does Keeley tell Roy she wants to happen to her body when she dies?

4. How much money does Rupert donate to the cause at Rebecca's first charity event in season one?

5. What is the name of the "trick play" which Richmond use to equalise against Manchester City in the final game of season one?

6. What insulting gift does Roy's niece receive from Bernard, a boy at her school?

7. How many players does Nate substitute when calling his game-winning play against Spurs?

8. Which stadium do Richmond and Manchester City play their FA Cup semi final at?

9. Who is the first person to guess Rebecca is dating Sam?

10. Who scored the first (and, as of the end of season two, only) AFC Richmond hat-trick featured in the show?

Answers on page 77

AFC Richmond

1. What is the club's nickname?

2. What is the name of the club's ground?

3. In which year was the club founded?

4. Who scored the goal that relegated Richmond on the last day of the season in series one?

5. Which club figure hosts Christmas dinner for players unable to get home to their families?

6. How many consecutive matches did Richmond draw before at the start of the Championship season in series two?

7. What was the name of the club's animal mascot?

8. And who accidentally killed that mascot during a match?

9. What is the name of the Richmond sponsor which Sam inspires the team to cover up on their jerseys?

10. And which brand replaces them as shirt sponsor?

Answers on page 78

Shirt Numbers

Which players wear the following shirt numbers for Richmond?

24?

9?

81?

6?

14?

5?

12?

21?

13?

2?

Answers on page 79

General Knowledge

1. What does Sharon's pinball high-score handle, "SMF", apparently stand for?

2. Who Facetimes into Rebecca's dad's funeral?

3. When Beard introduces himself to the university guys as Professor Declan Patrick Aloysius MacManus, which singer's real name is he actually using?

4. The 'Ted' in Ted Lasso is short for which name?

5. What film is Ted watching on Christmas Day when Rebecca turns up to rescue him from spending the day on his own?

6. Richmond's ground is affectionately known by what nickname?

7. Who scored the winning goal against Everton in season one?

8. Where does Ted get the biscuits he gives to Rebecca each morning?

9. Who is the only other person in the show Ted has offered those biscuits to?

10. In which year did season one first air?

Answers on page 80

Complete the Quote

1. "Football is _____!" - Dani.

2. "I never know how to react when a grown man _____ in front of me." - Keeley.

3. "Old people are so wise. They're like tall _____." - Jamie.

4. "You had me at _____." - Roy.

5. "[Jamie and Dani], they're artists. And, Colin, you paint too, but your work doesn't end up in museums. It hangs at... Well, you're like a painting at a _____ _____." - Nate.

6. "Well, I can't be your mentor without occasionally being your _____." - Sharon.

7. "That Rebecca is an intimidating and very _____ woman." - Keeley.

8. "I never know how to react when a grown man does the _____ in front of me." - Roy.

9. "Cheer up, Keeley. It's a _____." - Roy.

10. "I don't drink coffee. My mother always says I was born
_____." - Dani.

Answers on page 81

Cast and Crew

1. Who created the show?

2. Who plays Ted Lasso?

3. Who plays Rebecca?

4. Who plays Higgins?

5. Who plays Jamie?

6. Who plays Roy?

7. Who plays Coach Beard?

8. Who plays Nate?

9. Who plays Keeley?

10. Who plays Dr. Sharon Fieldstone?

11. Who plays Sam?

12. Who plays Trent Crimm?

13. Who plays Jane?

14. Who plays Rupert?

15. Which member of a 2013 Glastonbury headlining band co-wrote the theme tune with Tom Howe?

Answers on page 82

Complete the Quote - Ted Special

1. "I do love a locker room. It smells like _____." - Ted.

2. "You know what the happiest animal on Earth is? It's a _____." - Ted.

3. "I always thought tea was going to taste like _____ _____ _____. And do you know what? I was right." - Ted.

4. "Ice cream is the best. It's kinda like seeing _____ _____ perform live. Never disappoints." - Ted.

5. "There's two buttons I never like to hit: that's panic and _____." - Ted.

6. "If God would have wanted games to end in a tie, she wouldn't have invented _____." - Ted.

7. "This woman is strong, confident, and powerful. Boss, I tell you, I'd hate to see you and _____ _____ arm wrestle, but I wouldn't be able to take my eyes off of it, either." - Ted.

8. "Sam was more open than the jar of _____ _____ on my counter." - Ted.

9. "You could fill two _____ with what I don't know about football." - Ted.

10. "Our goal is to go out like _____ _____ - on a high!" - Ted.

Answers on page 84

General Knowledge

1. What are the names of the duo who provide the TV commentary for most of Richmond's matches?

2. What was the name of Higgins' old cat?

3. During their run of drawn matches, Richmond receive a giant food delivery from rivals Brentford FC. What type of food is it?

4. What is the name of Rupert's girlfriend?

5. According to Ted, why should one never accept a candy bar from little Ronnie Fouch?

6. What activity does Roy take part in with a group of sixty-something women?

7. What age was Ted when his father died?

8. What was the name of the club Beard managed to trick his (and three Richmond fans) way into?

9. If Rupert had beaten Ted at darts, what would Rupert have won?

10. What is the name of the new kitman who replaces Nate following his promotion to coach?

Answers on page 85

Production

1. On which streaming service did the show first appear?

2. The first shot of Ted in the series shows him celebrating with his former American football team while doing the Running Man dance. On what show had Jason Sudeikis previously performed this dance?

3. Which member of the cast has actually played for a professional football team?

4. Disney originally blocked the show from including 'Let It Go'. What was the fallback option for Rebecca to perform at karaoke?

5. Which four cast members are also on the writing team for the show?

6. AFC Richmond's home stadium is actually which real-life club's ground?

7. Which *Scrubs* actor directed episode two of *Ted Lasso*?

8. As of the end of season two, who has directed the most episodes of *Ted Lasso*?

9. Who directed the first episode of *Ted Lasso*?

10. Who does Jason Sudeikis credit with first coming up with the idea for the show, back in 2015?

Answers on page 86

Trivia

1. *Ted Lasso* broke the record for most Emmy nominations for a new comedy series. How many nominations did it get for its first Emmys?

2. Which real footballer is the character of Roy Kent based on?

3. The Latin motto of AFC Richmond, as shown on the dressing room walls is "Gradarius Firmus Victoria". What does this translate to?

4. Jason Sudeikis first portrayed the character of Ted Lasso in a series of ads for which network's coverage of the Premier League?

5. In those promos, which Premier League team had apparently hired Ted as their manager?

6. Nick Mohammed, who plays Nate, originally auditioned to play which other character?

7. Phil Dunster, who plays Jamie, originally auditioned to play which other character?

8. Which former X Factor contestant cameos as the host of *Lust Conquers All*, the reality dating show on which Jamie appears?

9. Cristo Fernández, who plays Dani Rojas, was originally intended to play which character?

10. Which Premier League referee makes a cameo appearance in the series, showing a yellow card to Nate for touchline abuse?

Answers on page 87

Sacrifices

Can you name the player by the item they sacrificed to rid the stadium's treatment room of its 'curse'?

1. A blanket given to him by his grandad?

2. A picture of the 1994 Nigerian World Cup team?

3. Sunglasses a girl once complimented him on, saying that he looked like Clive Owen?

4. A *Deadpool* figurine?

5. Sand from the beach on which he first slept with a supermodel?

6. A recent, unflattering newspaper article?

7. The only pen he could use to write his name with when he was younger?

8. His deceased cat's collar?

9. Lamborghini keys?

10. Football boots given to him by his mum?

Answers on page 88

General Knowledge

1. What was the name of the sports psychologist who joined Richmond in series two?

2. What was the score in the FA Cup semi final that Richmond lost to Manchester City?

3. Before beating Everton in season one, how long was it since Richmond had recorded their previous victory against the same opposition?

4. Who cut Sam's hair before his first date with Rebecca?

5. When coaching, what does Roy do instead of using a whistle?

6. Following Ted's early exit from the FA Cup sixth round match due to a panic attack, what is the cover story he gives as an explanation?

7. Which artist does Edwin apparently introduce Sam to at the museum in season two?

8. While playing (/hustling) Rupert at darts, Ted references a Walt Whitman quote he saw once. What is the quote?

9. When Ted says, "Sam and Rebecca are already one of my all-time favorite TV couples," which television show is he referring to?

10. Can you name the six *Ted Lasso* actors and actresses nominated for a best supporting role award at the 2021 Emmys?

Answers on page 89

Ted Lasso in Numbers

1. How much did Jamie sell for at the player auction during the charity fundraising event?

2. How much did Roy sell for at the same auction?

3. What does Ted score with his last three darts to beat Rupert in their pub wager?

4. In which year did the Ted Lasso character first appear on-screen?

5. How many people does AFC Richmond's ground hold?

6. As of season two, how long has Higgins been married to his wife?

7. What percentage stake in AFC Richmond does Rupert's girlfriend buy during season one?

8. At what age did Ted start playing darts each week at a sports bar with his father?

9. According to Nate, how many miles from his wife and child did Ted move when he joined Richmond?

10. In total, how many episodes were there in the first two series of *Ted Lasso*?

Answers on page 90

ANSWERS

Answer Sheet: Ted

1. The D.

2. Crystal Palace.

3. Kansas.

4. Henry.

5. A drone.

6. Michelle.

7. Tottenham Hotspur.

8. Snooker. He'd love to curl up under a weighted blanket and enjoy a box of snookers.

9. Wichita State University.

10. "Barbecue sauce".

Answer Sheet: Roy

1. His eyebrows.

2. Phoebe.

3. Sunderland.

4. Chelsea.

5. *A Wrinkle In Time* by Madeleine L'Engle.

6. *The Da Vinci Code.*

7. Ms. Bowen.

8. Isaac.

9. White orchids.

10. Reba McEntire.

Answer Sheet: Nate

1. Kitman.

2. Taste of Athens.

3. A Mini.

4. .001 miles tall.

5. Park the bus.

6. Wonder Kid.

7. A whistle.

8. Their 35th, or Jade wedding anniversary.

9. A tiger, so that he could ravage anybody who looked at him wrong,

10. Keeley.

Answer Sheet: Beard

1. 'Bad Romance'.

2. Oxford University.

3. Gary Lineker and Thierry Henry.

4. Jane.

5. Chess.

6. Margaret.

7. Two. One night is good, two is perfect, three is too many.

8. Meeting somebody's parents.

9. Horses and radishes. (But not horseradish.)

10. At a pagan ritual at Stonehenge.

Answer Sheet: Keeley

1. A lion.

2. A panda.

3. Liverpool.

4. *Sex and the City.*

5. The post-match interview from his final game where he is sobbing.

6. *Vanity Fair.*

7. The boot room.

8. Sexy Christmas.

9. Mushrooms. Because if you leave them in the dark they just get bigger.

10. A service station.

Answer Sheet: Sam

1. Nigeria.

2. 'Wonderwall' by Oasis.

3. Renee Zellweger. Specifically in the Bridget Jones movies.

4. LDN152.

5. 152 Wargrave Square, SW11.

6. Chin chin.

7. *Harry Potter*.

8. *Ratatouille*.

9. Right back.

10. He gives it back to Ted, on account of the toy's ties to American imperialism.

Answer Sheet: Rebecca

1, Bossgirl.

2. Le Tucci.

3. 'Let It Go'.

4. 'Never Gonna Give You Up'.

5. Stinky.

6. The 10th Annual Benefit for Underprivileged Children.

7. Robbie Williams.

8. "Old Rebecca".

9. A rickshaw.

10. Deborah.

Answer Sheet: Jamie

1. Manchester City.

2. 51.

3. James Tartt.

4. George Harrison.

5. They all give him the finger.

6. *Lust Conquers All.*

7. Chewing gum.

8. Vanilla vodka. "Such a child."

9. Darsteiner.

10. "Arm".

Answer Sheet: Higgins

1. Director of Communications. He then graduated to become Director of Football Operations.

2. Leslie. It was his mother's name. He's what's known as a 'feminine junior'.

3. The jazz bass.

4. Five - Terry, Kris, Dana, Stevie and Lindsay.

5. He is a priest (but a cool one).

6. They found a little bit of glass in the pasta.

7. Sciatica.

8. Van Dyke, named after a 17th century Flemish painter.

9. Julie.

10. 'She's a Rainbow' by The Rolling Stones.

Answer Sheet: General Knowledge

1. Mexico.

2. The Independent.

3. Edwin Akufo.

4. Raja Casablanca.

5. What song does Ted have the team practicing a dance to for Sharon's leaving party? Bye Bye Bye by NSYNC.

6. The Crown & Anchor.

7. Mae.

8. Sam's.

9. Sassy.

10. The Diamond Dogs. Alternative names included "Ted Lasso's Personal Dilemma Squad", "The E.Q. Warriors", and "The Proud Boys".

Answer Sheet: Anagrams

1. A Noisy Samba = Sam Obisanya.

2. Tory Ken = Roy Kent.

3. A Jam Titter = Jamie Tartt.

4. Charade Cob = Coach Beard.

5. So Salted = Ted Lasso.

6. A Concrete Blew = Rebecca Welton.

7. Eek Enjoys El = Keeley Jones.

8. A Prominent Urn = Rupert Mannion.

9. Siege Shilling = Leslie Higgins.

10. Heal Tensely = Nate Shelley.

11. Mr Cent Trim = Trent Crimm.

12. Net Foolhardiness = Sharon Fieldstone.

13. Fills Colon = Flo Collins.

14. Aide Wok Fun = Edwin Akufo.

15. Hyena Ruler Dog = Earl Greyhound.

Answer Sheet: Trick Plays

1. The Belgian Deadline? False.

2. Beckham's Todger? True.

3. Code Beaujolais? False.

4. Frightshaft? False.

5. Lasso Special? True.

6. Loki's Toboggan? True.

7. Hadrian's Wall? True.

8. The Broken Tap? True.

9. The Upside Down Taxi? True.

10. Nakatomi Plaza? False.

11. The Satin Chokey? False.

12. Chitty Chitty Bang Bang? True.

---

13. The Jealous Heron? False.

14. Land of Hope and Glory? False.

15. Midnight Poutine? True.

16. The Baffler? False.

17. Rupert's Lament? False.

18. Dirty Martini? True.

19. Gentle Bailiff? False.

20. The Queen's Gambit? False.

Answer Sheet: General Knowledge

1. Diane.

2. She ate her placenta. Raw. And the baby knows it.

3. She wants to be buried in a biodegradable sack in which her body will fertilise the seeds of a fruit tree. Then she wants all of the people that love her to eat the fruit from the tree. (Roy: That's f*cking mental.)

4. One million pounds. Such a great guy.

5. The Lasso Special.

6. Toothpaste and mouthwash.

7. Three. Colin, Dani and Richard.

8. Wembley Stadium.

9. Keeley.

10. Sam.

Answer Sheet: AFC Richmond

1. The Greyhounds.

2. Nelson Road.

3. 1897.

4. Hendricks of Manchester City.

5. Higgins.

6. Eight.

7. Earl Greyhound.

8. Dani Rojas, with a drilled penalty.

9. Dubai Air.

10. Bantr.

Answer Sheet: Shirt Numbers

24 is Sam.

9 is Jamie Tartt.

81 is Zoreaux.

6 is Roy.

14 is Dani Rojos.

5 is Isaac Macadoo.

12 is Colin Hughes.

21 is Moe Bumbercatch.

13 is Jan Maas.

2 is Arlo Dixon.

Answer Sheet: General Knowledge

1. "Sexy Motherf*cker".

2. Jane.

3. Elvis Costello.

4. Theodore.

5. *It's a Wonderful Life.*

6. The Dogtrack.

7. Roy Kent.

8. He bakes them himself.

9. Sharon.

10. 2020.

Answer Sheet: Complete the Quote

1. Life.

2. Beatboxes.

3. Yodas.

4. Coach.

5. Holiday Inn.

6. Tormentor.

7. Tall.

8. Carlton.

9. Funeral.

10. Caffeinated.

Answer Sheet: Cast and Crew

1. Bill Lawrence.

2. Jason Sudeikis.

3. Hannah Waddingham.

4. Jeremy Swift.

5. Phil Dunster.

6. Brett Goldstein.

7. Brendan Hunt.

8. Nick Mohammed.

9. Juno Temple.

10. Sarah Niles.

11. Toheeb Jimoh.

12. James Lance.

13. Phoebe Walsh.

14. Anthony Head.

15. Marcus Mumford.

Answer Sheet: Complete the Quote - Ted Special

1. Potential.

2. Goldfish.

3. Hot brown water.

4. Billy Joel.

5. Snooze.

6. Numbers.

7. Michelle Obama.

8. Peanut butter.

9. Internets.

10. Willie Nelson.

Answer Sheet: General Knowledge

1. Arlo White and Chris Powell.

2. Cindy Clawford.

3. Thai.

4. Bex.

5. Because there's a good chance that little son of a gun has pooped inside of a Butterfinger wrapper. No one ever saw him do it, but a couple people ate it.

6. Yoga.

7. 16.

8. Bones and Honey.

9. Ted would have let Rupert choose the Richmond lineup for the last two games of the season.

10. Will.

Answer Sheet: Production

1. Apple TV+.

2. *Saturday Night Live.*

3. Cristo Fernández, who appears as Dani Rojas, and who previously played for Tescos FC in Mexico.

4. 'I Will Survive' by Gloria Gaynor.

5. Jason Sudeikis, Brett Goldstein, Brendan Hunt and Phoebe Walsh.

6. Selhurst Park, the real life ground of Crystal Palace.

7. Zach Braff. He was in London anyway so Bill Lawrence roped him in.

8. Declan Lowney. He also directed the 1988 Eurovision Song Contest.

9. Tom Marshall.

10. Olivia Wilde.

Answer Sheet: Trivia

1. 20.

2. Roy Keane, formerly of Nottingham Forest, Manchester United, Celtic and Ireland.

3. "Slow and steady wins the race."

4. NBC Sports.

5. Tottenham Hotspur.

6. Higgins.

7. Also Higgins. Popular role!

8. Fleur East.

9. Jamie Tartt. (Jamie's character was initially planned to be Latin American.)

10. Mike Dean.

Answer Sheet: Sacrifices

1. Roy.

2. Sam.

3. Nate.

4. Zoreaux.

5. Richard Montlaur.

6. Rebecca.

7. Isaac.

8. Higgins.

9. Colin.

10. Jamie.

Answer Sheet: General Knowledge

1. Dr. Sharon Fieldstone.

2. 0-6.

3. 60 years.

4. Isaac.

5. He shouts "WHISTLE". Because actual whistles give his mouth hives.

6. He claims he had a case of food poisoning.

7. Banksy.

8. "Be curious."

9. *Cheers*.

10. Hannah Waddingham (Rebecca), Juno Temple (Keeley), Brett Goldstein (Roy), Jeremy Swift (Higgins), Nick Mohammed (Nate) and Brendan Hunt (Beard).

Answer Sheet: Ted Lasso in Numbers

1. £25,000.

2. £6,000.

3. 170. Two treble twenties and a bullseye.

4. 2012.

5. 25,456.

6. 29 years.

7. 2.9%.

8. Ten.

9. 4,438.

10. Twenty-two.

Thanks for playing, quizzer! If you've enjoyed the book, please leave a review on Amazon: it only takes a minute and it really helps! Take care.

- Alex.

OTHER BOOKS BY ALEX MITCHELL

Quizzin' Nine-Nine: A *Brooklyn Nine-Nine* Quiz Book

Parks & Interrogation: A *Parks & Recreation* Quiz Book

Q & AC-12: A *Line of Duty Quiz* Book

Know Your Schitt: A *Schitt's Creek* Quiz Book

Examilton: A *Hamilton* Quiz Book

Stranger Thinks: A *Stranger Things* Quiz Book

The El Clued Brothers: A *Peep Show* Quiz Book

Dunder Quizlin: An *Office US* Quiz Book

A Question of Succession: A *Succession* Quiz Book

The Big Bang Queries: A *Big Bang Theory* Quiz Book

The Greendale Study Guide: A *Community* Quiz Book

Know Your Schmidt: A *New Girl* Quiz Book

Les Quizérables: *A Les Misérables* Quiz Book

Dunphy or Dunce? A *Modern Family* Quiz Book

Printed in Great Britain
by Amazon